for my dear son Markus

and all the birthday girls and boys out there

Bibliographical Information, The German National Library: The German National Library registered this publication in the German National Bibliography; detailed bibliographic information is available at http://dnb.ddb.de.

ISBN 978-3-7448-8156-2

Other English parents´ guides and family books of Ayleen Lyschamaya:
- *EMDR for Babies*
- *Spiritual Psychotherapy: the inner family*

German Edition 2007: *Harmonischer Kindergeburtstag, Kindergeburtstage ohne Verlierer, Gemeinschaftsfördernde Gruppenspiele*

1. English edition 2010 ISBN 978-3-8391-7076-2
translated by S.T. Paterson
© 2010 Dr. Ayleen Birgit Scheffler-Hadenfeldt

2. English edition 2019 ISBN 978-3-7448-8156-2
additional translation by Ayleen Lyschamaya
© 2019 Ayleen Lyschamaya

Production and Publication: Books on Demand GmbH, Norderstedt.

Contents

	Page
Why Choose Non-Competitive Games?	4
Children's Birthday as Inner Family Birthday Party	5
Non-Competitive Games	7
Prizes	7
Free Play	9
Playful Battle	9
Determining Turns and Pairs	10
Quiet, More Energetic and Rough-and-Tumble Games	11
Water Games	27
Fantasy and Story Games	33
Food Games	41
Painting and Crafts	45
Magic	48
Keep it Casual	49
Consider the Age of the Children	51
Build up the Suspense	54
Themed Birthdays	56
Pirates	56
Rally	58
Horses	59
How to Lead Non-Competitive Games Convincingly	61
Develop Your Own Non-Competitive Games	63
Hints and Tips for a Successful Birthday Party	65
Acknowledgements	69
Ayleen Lyschamaya	70
Games Index	74

Why Choose Non-Competitive Games?

Many adults find it difficult not to be a bad loser – and it is even more difficult for children who have yet to learn how to lose. However, the art of losing should not be taught on birthdays, as these should be very special celebrations with lots of happiness, fun and a merry atmosphere.

 In traditional competitive games such as sack racing or egg and spoon races, children are pitted against each other to create winners and losers. Non-competitive games on the other hand avoid competition and instead often require teamwork. They produce a largely imperceptible – but very important – mood of community spirit, while competitive games simply bring out conflict among birthday guests.

In this book, I would first like to introduce you to different non-competitive birthday games, followed by advice on how you yourself can develop your own. Some useful tips will also be provided, as illustrated in a description of a successful sixth birthday party.

Children's Birthday as Inner Family Birthday Party

How you experience the preparation of a child's birthday, depends largely on your own inner family. The human psyche consists of an inner family with inner child, inner woman and inner man, which are mirrored by outer experiences and thus made conscious.

For example, if you are uncomfortable hosting a child's birthday party, it will be up to your inner family members. Maybe your inner man is not involved enough, so that the organization is difficult for you. Or perhaps your inner woman is overburdened with caring for everyone. In addition, your inner child may have learned not to be the centre of attention, so you also don't like to make your birthday child the centre of attention. It is definitely worthwhile to think about your own inner family, because then you can directly address your inner family members inwardly and thus positively change your attitude towards children's birthdays.

If, on the other hand, you enjoy hosting a children's birthday party, you only have to make sure that your own inner child also takes part in it. In this way you do yourself good and radiate a warm welcome energetically to your birthday child and the guests. Just act as if there is another birthday guest, your own inner child.

Also your basic attitude towards the birthday games is shaped by your inner family and its experiences. Inner children are looking for love and want to please. Inner women wish for harmony and have the ability to work in a team. Inner men delimit themselves and compete with others. This means that your inner child and your inner woman like non-competitive group games, while your inner man prefers competitive games. Therefore, you should let your inner man step into the background when choosing and guiding the games.

Why should the selection and instruction of the birthday games be directed towards the inner child and the inner woman instead of the inner man? Because this corresponds to the natural human development. Until puberty, the inner child and then the inner woman develop one after the other in the human psyche. Thus, the inner child and the inner woman are in the foreground for the period of time that these birthday games are about. If their needs are met, this promotes the development of your child and her or his birthday guests. The important ability to work in a team is acquired.

So, if you let your inner child and your inner woman be responsible for the birthday games and hand over the organisation to your inner man, the children's birthday will give you a lot of joy and at the same time you will promote the development of the children.

However, please do not regard the contact with your inner family as an additional burden and further requirement to be fulfilled, but instead consider it a playful discovery. It is only a matter of getting to know yourself a little better, understanding your own behaviour more than before and becoming aware of your inner influence on external situations. In the following I will therefore in some places remind you, which inner family members are particularly addressed.

Non-Competitive Games

Some more general comments on prizes, free play, playful battle, turn-taking and pairs will precede a description of popular non-competitive games. For easy categorisation, they are classified into sections: quiet, more energetic and rough-and-tumble games, water games, fantasy and story games, food games, painting and crafts, as well as magic. Any original traditional competitive games are marked in *italics*, with a description of the modified non-competitive game afterwards.

Prizes

In competitive games, the winner usually receives a prize while the other children finish empty-handed. In non-competitive games, however, each child gets a small surprise for his or her participation in the group activity – albeit only awarded in some games.

I always buy prizes over the course of the year so that I don't have to go shopping just before the actual event. Suitable prizes are, for example, pretty stickers on the children's special interests (horses, ball sports) and special pens and pencils (glitter pens, multicoloured felt-tip pens, etc.). Younger children are also very happy with plastic watches, proudly wearing their new timepieces just like mum and dad. Large bargain packs containing children's party items like yo-yos, patience games, helicopters, water pistols, bouncy balls, puzzles and much more are commonly available.

I frequently select small surprises that can be incorporated into the birthday set-up. For example, children of kindergarten age received bottles of soap bubbles during Beat the Pot, after which they were able to try it out during free play. In order not to ruin the cooperative spirit it is important to begin free play only when the previous game is over and everyone has got a prize.

Six-year-old children were so excited with their small planes to be shot with elastic bands that they were employed for a longer period of time.

When offering these sorts of prizes, please remember to provide some replacement elastic.

Animals can be made out of model balloons, but our children were overwhelmingly in favour of swords that they could use straightaway in playful battle. Modelling Balloons is not particularly easy for children (or indeed many adults), so a well-practised person should be present to take on this task.

An equal amount of ammunition for a confetti pistol was also distributed to each child as a prize, so that there was no dispute as to who was allowed to shoot or how often.

Lastly, we give out party bags containing more small surprises in order to ease the children's departure: these may only be opened once the children have left the party. To make them even more exciting, we put them on a table and draw lots to award them. As all the party bags look the same, there are no disappointments – instead each and every draw is a happy bonus.

Reminder: When you host a children's birthday party, you are not only dealing with your birthday child and her or his guests, but also with your own inner child. In order for you to create a real psychological-energetic welcome for children, please also deal well with your own inner child. This means that all prices you give to the children should also be given to your own inner child.

You can learn more about the healing treatment of your own inner child in my basic book "Spiritual Psychotherapy: the inner family".

Free Play

If free play occurs spontaneously among the children, be happy and simply go with the flow. I also find free play important in order not to overwhelm the children with too many structured games. Of course, I like to make a birthday celebration special, something out of the ordinary. So, I use guided games and free play alternating. The free play phases I arrange to coincide with trying out the prizes, organise freer games such as water fights and add surprises into the mix.

For example, my son was utterly enthralled by a soap bubble gun, which the children could take turns at shooting while the remaining guests tried to catch the bubbles. Confetti pistols are fun especially for the older children, but are limited in their ammunition and require later removal of the confetti.

Remember that free play is more likely to arise, and go on for longer, in relatively homogenous groups where the children know each other. In groups where the children are unfamiliar with each other, you will probably require more structured games.

Playful Battle

Perhaps it strikes you as odd that I write rather a lot about fights, pistols and battles for a book on non-competitive games. Yet play fights are typical for boys, while there are usually no 'fights' on girls' birthdays.

I distinguish between playful battle in free play and guided competitive games: in a spontaneous sword or newspaper battle, for example, it is all about the fun of the fight – and there is no loser. Competitive games focus on winning, not on the game itself. The other child becomes a competitor, and this time there is a loser.

Determining Turns and Pairs

In some games, the children take turns, or require a partner. At our parties, the birthday child always starts and the other children usually organise their own sequence, or accept what you decide. They also usually manage to find a partner without any problems. However, if you would like to make this process more interesting and leave it to chance, the children can draw lots with numbers or throw dice.

Lots: To determine the <u>sequence</u> by lots, begin with the number two if the birthday child is to start. To establish <u>pairs</u>, arrange two lots with the same number or symbol.

Dice: With dice, each child's <u>turn</u> results from the numbers rolled. To determine a <u>pair</u>, the children keep throwing the dice until two children roll the same number – they then form a pair. The other children keep playing until all children are matched up. Throwing a large foam dice instead of the traditional cube can also be a lot of fun.

Quiet, More Energetic and Rough-and-Tumble Games

The following games are arranged in ascending liveliness: from quiet games to more boisterous. However, how a game ultimately develops always depends on the real-life situation.

Chinese Whispers

Place: inside and outside
Material: -
Characteristics: very quiet, funny

The children sit or stand in a circle next to each other. One child invents a multiple-syllable word or a simple sentence and whispers it to his or her neighbour. The neighbour then whispers what he or she has understood to the next child, and so on. The last child voices what he or she has heard, while the first child then announces the starter word or sentence for comparison.

Secret Hand Pressure

Place: inside and outside
Material: -
Characteristics: very quiet, perception training

The children sit or stand in a circle. Their grabbed hands are visible. One child is in the middle of this circle. A hand pressure starts secretly transmitted from any circle child you nod to inconspicuously. It then goes on from one child to the next. The child in the middle must try to see the hand pressure and point at it. If the hand pressure is "caught", another child comes into the middle. You should take part in the game and, if necessary, get "caught deliberately" so as not to expose a child, who may not perceive the hand pressure so well.

Figuring out the Puzzle

Place: inside and outside
Material: dice, a small puzzle [another gift] per child
Characteristics: very quiet, skill in puzzles

At my son's seventh birthday I had the guests throw dice for small puzzles, in which several coloured balls had to be put into a certain sequence.

The children sat at a table and threw the dice in turn. A six got them their puzzle, which they were then able to try out immediately. After the first six had been thrown, I added more winning numbers to shorten the wait for the other children.

Not all children like puzzles, but in a group like this the other children's interest has a contagious effect. Of course, you can also dice another gift.

Pin the Tail on the Donkey

Age: kindergarten age
Place: inside and outside
Material: animal picture on cardboard, animal tail on a drawing pin, blindfold (e.g. scarf)
Characteristics: quiet game, funny

My son had fun helping me prepare this game for his fifth birthday. I drew the outline of a large horse on cardboard in black pen, while he coloured it in with crayon. For the animal's tail we fixed wrapping paper ribbons to a drawing pin. Blindfolded, each child was now able to

try to pinpoint the correct place for the animal's tail, with amusing results.

Note: If you want to give out prizes for this game, please do so for participation and not for accuracy.

Pass the Potato

Age: kindergarten age
Place: inside and outside
Material: one spoon per child, one to three potatoes [possibly tape]
Characteristics: high concentration, short duration

This is similar to an egg and spoon race, but in this game the children must balance a potato instead of an egg on their spoon. *In traditional egg and spoon races two children race each other along parallel tracks. Yet even the younger children soon begin comparing themselves and their abilities with each other.*

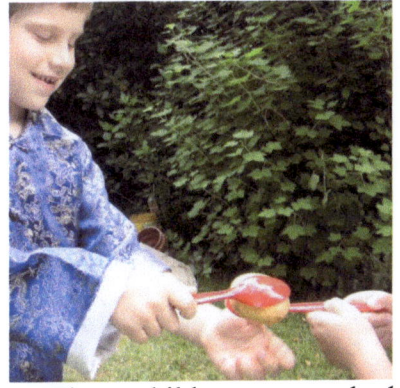

In the non-competitive variation, however, the children form a circle. If there is not enough space inside the room, the circle can also go around tables and chairs, or through several rooms. Marking the circle or circuit on the floor with tape is recommended for the purposes of orientation. All the children get a spoon, while the potatoes are distributed to one to three children standing apart.

These children move clockwise towards their neighbour balancing a potato and pass it from spoon to spoon without using the other hand. (Fallen potatoes can of course be picked up with the other hand.) The children stand on their new spot until they get the next potato and must pass it on.

As all the children are thoroughly occupied at the same time, nobody feels particularly scrutinised and it also removes any potential boredom from standing around doing nothing. Kindergarten children have fun overcoming such a difficult task together.

13

The game is over when this sense of fun starts to disappear and concentration skills dwindle. Don't demand too much of the children; instead ensure that the game ends on a note of success.

Catching Soap Bubbles

Age: the youngest children
Place: outside; also possible inside, but bear in mind possible stains
Material: soap bubbles
Characteristics: shimmering fascination

Catching soap bubbles is fun for very small children –

and the littlest ones will watch enraptured.

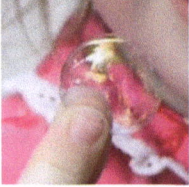 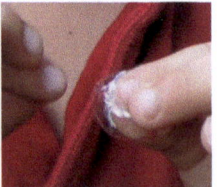

Incidentally, there are soap bubbles available for purchase that you can actually catch: they do not burst immediately.

Hideout Land

Age: kindergarten age
Place: inside [also possible outside, e.g. with chairs or bushes]
Material: tape, scissors, bed linen or old table cloths;
[possibly large cardboard boxes]
Characteristics: free hiding game, creative play (e.g. houses)

At our house, there is a section of hallway that is suitable for criss-crossing tape between several door handles and the radiators. This can then be used as the base on which to "build" a hideout land: sheets, light covers, towels or similar can be arranged in any old way over the tape lines (hanging over them or spread out like a roof). Large boxes, possibly with windows cut in, can also be set up.

14

If you do not have a spare room where the Hideout Land can be prepared as a surprise, involve the children in its construction. Before the party, think about where you would like to attach the tape and leave the sheets, etc. for the children to do. After their creative free play has come to an end, Hideout Land is very quick and easy to tidy up with a pair of scissors.

WARNING: Even if the little ones are playing nicely, never leave the children by themselves. If any tape comes unstuck, it could be dangerous.

Beat the Pot

Age: kindergarten age
Place: inside and outside
Material: saucepan, wooden spoon, blindfold, prize per child
[possibly additional spoons]
Characteristics: room orientation, can get noisy

One child at a time is blindfolded, given a wooden spoon and spun around so as to lose orientation. The pot is placed upside down, and a small surprise hidden underneath it. At the age of around five, children waiting for their turn enjoy doing this task together. The blindfolded child kneels down and crawls around trying to hit the saucepan with the wooden spoon. He or she gets the surprise present once he has successfully struck the pot. The other children help him find it with hints such as "cold", "warm", "warmer", "hot" and so on.

Tip: When there are lots of children, prevent boredom by letting the other children do more than just say "cold" and "warm". Give them something with which to tap on the saucepan (for example wooden bricks or spoons). The child searching thus finds the pot quicker and the communal noise makes it fun for the other children.

Blind Man's Buff

Place: inside and outside
Material: blindfold
Characteristics: sensory perception, tactile contact

A child is blindfolded as the 'blind man'. He or she now tries to catch another child – which is why the play area should not be too big. Once the 'blind man' has caught someone, he or she must guess who it is. To do so, they are allowed to feel their prisoner. If they guess correctly, the prisoner becomes the next 'blind man'.

Blowing Cotton Wool Balls

Place: inside and outside (not too windy) at a table
Material alternative 1: a straw per child, cotton wool, cardboard goals, toilet paper rolls, cartons or paper cups, colours (e.g. inks or paints), sellotape; [other popular craft materials]
Material alternative 2: one straw per child, cotton wool, Lego bricks
Characteristics: coordination skills

Traditionally, the children sit or stand around a table and blow one or several cotton wool balls with their straws (the game is sometimes also played without straws i.e. just by blowing). The aim is to blow the cotton wool balls off the table while ensuring that any balls in their particular vicinity are kept in the game: acting as goalkeepers, so to speak.

The non-competitive version of this needs a little preparation, but you can use the opportunity to turn it into a simple craft activity for you and your child.

Using the first set of materials, cardboard goals are cut out in different shapes and sizes. The goals, toilet paper rolls and cartons are then brightly painted. These pretty obstacles (which your child will certainly be proud of!) are taped to a table at the birthday party.

If using the second material alternative, you and your child can build the obstacles and mazes with Lego bricks, although naturally these can also be combined with the cardboard obstacles. Make enough obstacles so that all children can play at the same time, and ensure you offer various levels of difficulty. Also keep some free Lego bricks at the ready in case the children wish to alter the existing obstacles, or would like to add more.

Now give each child a straw and a cotton wool ball, which he or she must blow through the obstacles in any sequence. The cotton ball may also occasionally be sucked up in order to lift it. Before the game I usually advise the children that some around-the-corner-obstacles can only be conquered with a partner. They can also join forces in threes or fours.

Tip: Leave the obstacle table with the straws and cotton wool balls untouched for further free play. Some children may like to try again later.

Pass the Cotton Wool Ball
Place: inside and outside
Material: one straw per child, cotton wool
Characteristics: focused coordination and concentration, short duration

The children sit or stand in a circle. A cotton wool ball is given to every two or three children. The children suck the cotton ball with the straw and pass it to the straw of the neighbouring child. The cotton wool balls thus move around the circle from straw to straw.

Pass the Matchbox
Place: inside and outside
Material: matchbox lid
Characteristics: practising coordination in a comical way

Instead of using cotton balls as in the previous game, a matchbox lid can also be passed from nose to nose. Ensure that you try it out with your child before the birthday party to see if their noses are big enough to hold the matchbox lid reasonably well, otherwise the game will be too difficult.

Hit the Nail on the Head

Place: outside and inside
Material: thick wooden beam, various-sized nails, hammers
Characteristics: challenging handicrafts

In the competitive game, two children compete against each other to see who hammers his or her nail into the wooden beam the fastest.

Yet why should this be a competition? Just the hammering itself is a lot of fun for children aged about 6 to 8, so why not simply allow it? It can actually be quite difficult to hit an ordinary nail, so how would it work with nails of various sizes? As many children as there are hammers and space at the beam can participate at the same time. Taking turns is easy: Once a child has successfully hit in their nail, they simply pass their hammer to someone else.

Note: Please ensure that the beam is arranged in such a way that a miss-hit nail will not damage anything or anyone. You should also check to see whether any nails are lying on the floor afterwards.

Hanging up Laundry

Age: small children
Place: outside and inside
Material: clothesline, clothespins, (doll-)clothes
Characteristics: skillfulness

It is fun for small children to hang up laundry, because it is not so easy. To offer this practice, stretch a clothesline at a comfortable height for the children and provide laundry and clothespins. Whether you offer adult laundry, doll clothes or even wet laundry is up to you. Maybe you want to provide a selection.

Note: Please stay with the children as a supervisor in case the clothesline comes loose.

Speed Snake

Place: inside and outside
Material: - [perhaps blindfolds]
Characteristics: coordination challenge

The children line up and put their hands on the shoulder of the child standing in front. They now try to walk in step. The child at the front decides the varying speeds and directions: the line could go sideward or backwards, or even come to an abrupt stop. After a while, the child in front should go to the back of the line and the next child will determine the speed.

Game variant 1 (outside): For more boisterous children, this alternative involves more intensive movement and requires less concentration. This time, the children are not linked up – the child at the head of the line runs, jumps, waves their arms about ... and the other children copy. This can reduce excess energy, but can also boost it.

Game variant 2: The game can be played more calmly if the children are blindfolded.

Flying Balloons

Place: inside and outside
Material: balloons
Characteristics: community task, getting to know each other

Balloons are thrown into the air and the children must work together to ensure that they don't touch the floor. Thereby, the balloons must not be caught, but only pushed. The number of balloons depends on the size of the group and the children's ages. It might be best to judge the number by introducing balloons gradually, one after the other. You can also set goals, for example keeping as many balloons afloat as possible for as long as possible (or a set number thereof).

Flying Balloons is particularly good for the start of a party as it gradually involves the shyer children: the line between joining in and looking on from the outside gradually becomes blurred.

Balloon Footy

Place: inside and outside
Material: one balloon; [replacement balloons]
Characteristics: cooperative skill

The children sit spaced out on the floor and stretch their feet into the air. They may also move in spider mode (on all fours with their belly facing upward). Their joint task is to keep a balloon in the air using only their feet; without using their hands or other parts of the body. This is easier without shoes.

After a while, call a guest's name. At this point the balloon is passed to this child, who catches the balloon between his or her feet. Then he or she calls the next name and the balloon is now kicked to this child. Ensure that all children have the same length turn. At least three children must have kicked on the balloon (count together out loud) before it can be caught.

Unravelling a Human Ball of Thread

Place: inside and outside
Material: -
Characteristics: getting closer with funny results

A child must disentangle a 'ball of thread' consisting of the other children.

To do this, the children form a human pile by lying higgledy-piggedly across each other in all directions, their arms and legs inter-laced. When the ball is finished, the children may no longer move. The 'unraveller' must now disentangle the ball by calling instructions, for example "Anna, put your left arm up", "Marcus, take your right leg away" ...

Sort Chaos Circle

Place: inside and outside
Material: -
Characteristics: getting closer with funny results

 One child must sort the circle of chaos consisting of the other children. The other children form a circle and hold hands. Without letting go of each other, the children now climb through each other over and under each other's arms and legs. When the mess is as great as possible, the children are no longer allowed to move. The outside child must now sort out the chaos by telling individual children to climb over and under arms and legs. Once again, the children are not allowed to let each other go.

Music Stop

Place: inside and outside

Material: music

Characteristics: fun, the selection of music and task itself can be calming or stimulating depending on what you want

The children dance or move around to music. When the music stops, the children complete a little task. Younger children find it quite demanding to join up in twos, threes or fours and keep dancing together. Please ensure that no child is left out. If the birthday guests don't yet know each other, they should say their names. If they are relatively well-acquainted, however, a child may close his eyes and be guided by a second child. Then they change over.

The children could make a conga line or move backwards. Let the children grunt like pigs, gallop like horses, hop like frogs or crow like roosters. You can also clap a song (or let the birthday child clap), which the kids should guess. There are no limits to the imagination.

Spin the Bottle

Place: inside and outside

Material: plastic bottle

Characteristics: fun at creative tasks

The children sit in a circle around a bottle. *Traditionally, a child thinks up a task, and then spins the bottle. The child to whom the bottle head points must perform this task, after which the whole process is repeated.*

In the non-competitive alternative, the bottle determines the child that thinks up a task to be carried out by the rest of the group. This encourages shy children to play, and all children are occupied at the same time. The child who invents the task also joins in so that overly difficult tasks are avoided. The birthday child spins the bottle to start the game, thus selecting the first task-giver, but at all other times the bottle is spun by the task-giver.

Most children have spontaneous brainwaves, but if not you can of course step in with ideas – for example suggest the children move in spider mode (on all fours, belly upward), do star jumps, or sing a song together.

Opening Presents

  Place: inside and outside
  Material: plastic bottle, presents brought by the guests
  Characteristics: appreciation of the presents

You can also organise a game for everyone that involves opening the presents brought by the guests. Spin a bottle, and the person it points to gives his or her present to the birthday child. All children watch as the birthday boy or girl unwraps it, so that each present is shown off. The bottle is spun again until all presents are opened.

Wrap the Mummy

  Place: inside and outside
  Material: one roll of toilet paper per child
  Characteristics: funny transformations, skill

In pairs, one child stands still while the other child wraps him or her in toilet paper. Then they change round. Give the children the time they need without making the game a *speed contest*. It might be best to let the children that have already paired up start immediately: this staggered start ensures that they do not start to compare each other.

If there are an odd number of children, make sure that no child is left out by joining in yourself (or another adult). There is a lot of fun to be had, especially if all the children get together to wrap you – as game leader – up yourself!

  But please don't just join in for the love of the children. Instead, try to sense your own

23

inner child and really feel true joy yourself.

Clearing away the shredded toilet paper could also turn into a fun fight that finally ends with all the toilet paper in the bin.

Sardines

Place: inside and outside
Material: -
Characteristics: communal fun

One child – the sardine – hides, while the other children shut their eyes (no cheating) and slowly count to twenty. Then they all set off by themselves in search of the sardine. The sardine should not choose a hiding place that is too narrow, because the next child to discover him will join him in the hiding place. The third child to appear also squeezes in, and so on. The hidden children gradually become packed as tightly as sardines in a tin. Yet even with all the pushing and squeezing, the children should stay quiet so that those still searching don't hear them.

When a child has discovered the sardine(s), he or she must join them as unobtrusively as possible so that the other children do not notice.

Strung!

Games leader: should like puzzle games
Age: older children
Place: inside and outside
Material: tape, scissors
Characteristics: amusing, challenging

Strung! is a game for older children and can only be played once until the children work out the solution. Cut some string into strips about 1.3 – 1.5m long for each child depending on their size. The children then form pairs.

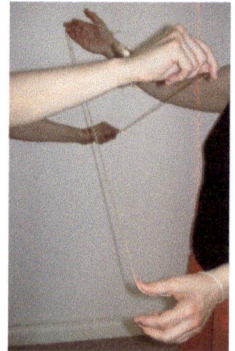

Tie each end of the string around each of one child's wrists. Pass the second string behind the first (now tied) string and tie each end to each of the second child's wrists, as before. Both children should now be connected as in the photo, forming two circles like chain links.

The children's task is to free themselves from one another. It really does work!

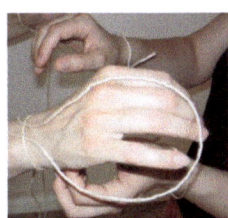

Solution: Make a loop with the first child's string and pass it through the string fixing it at the wrist of the second child, moving from back to front (i.e. pulling it towards the first child). Now pass the loop over the second child's hand. Then the loop has to be passed through the string knot once again, this time moving from front to back.

If you now pull the loop, both children should be separated from one another. Please try the solution beforehand because it is not that simple.

Please note: If the children have got completely entangled in their wild and comical attempts, the solution will no longer work. Only scissors will help in this case!

Balloon Stomp

Place: outside and inside
Material: balloons
Characteristics: fun, can dissipate aggression

Traditionally, each child ties a balloon to his or her ankle and then tries to stomp as many other balloons as possible, keeping his or her own intact.

It need not be a case of "my balloon against yours" when the game is focused not on pitting yourself against others, but about the fun of the stomping. You and the children can blow up as many balloons as the group wants. After the start signal the balloons can then be stomped together – and all that popping is fun!

25

Keep your Distance

Number of children: lots of children
Place: outside
Material: -
Characteristics: imagination, movement

You and the children should decide on an area in which everyone may run about. Then each child should think of another child in the group, without revealing the name. They should keep as far away from this child as they can inside the pre-determined space. With enough children, the group will be in a state of permanent movement. Let the children stop from time to time to guess who thought of whom. Then it's off again with a new person in mind.

At the end of the game, you can gather the children together by changing the aim of the game from "utmost distance" to "as near the person as possible"!

Sack Races Tag

Place: outside, only possible inside with smaller children and larger spaces
Material: a large bin liner per child [have replacement bin liners ready]
Characteristics: uses up surplus energy, fun

In traditional sack races, two children (sometimes also in two teams) hop to the finish line, thus emphasising that there are winners and losers.

With the non-competitive principle, however, all children hop around in their sacks at the same time. Two children (who are "it") try to "tag" the other sack racers, who then become "it" in turn. With small numbers, only one child can be "it" and the space should be fairly small so that he or she is not over-strained.

Sack Races "Tag" is a lot of fun, and great at reducing surplus energy inside a relatively small space.

26

Sack Catchers

Place: outside, only possible inside with smaller children and larger spaces
Material: a large bin liner per child; [have replacement bin liners ready]
Characteristics: uses up surplus energy, fun

Sack Catchers works in a similar way to Sack Races Tag, except that all the children, not just one or two, must catch someone else. Call a child's name, and this child now hops away from the other children. To catch the child, a simple "tag" is not enough: the other children must surround the hopping child. Sometimes the children end up rolling around on top of each other! You can decide how far a child is chased by calling another name before the game becomes too wild. The escaping child also has a chance to "save" himself by calling a new name, if he or she decides they no longer want to be chased.

Tip: If you would like to offer both Sack Races Tag and Sack Catchers at the party, please ensure you have bin liners for each game as these may not last for both!

Water Games

You and your guests are likely to get wet in most of the following games, so please ask the guests to bring bathing costumes or a spare set of clothes with them. As a precaution, I usually make sure I have additional underwear to hand, which serve as swimming trunks in emergencies.

Waggle Balloon

Place: inside (with limited water risk) and outside
Material: two balloons to make one waggle balloon
Characteristics: unusual balloon experience, funny

A balloon is placed inside a second balloon with only its neck visible. This is then drawn over a narrow tap, filled with water and sealed. The second balloon is blown up with air and also sealed. The 'waggle balloon' is thus a small water-filled balloon inside a large balloon filled with air, which has an erratic flight path when thrown.

We played Waggle Balloon at the start of my son's seventh birthday to great success, as a playful way to pass the time before all the guests arrived.

Fireman´s Fun

Place: outside with tap/water supply
Material: hose, table (which you are happy to get wet), cans or plastic cups [possibly a blindfold]
Characteristics: fun, stimulating

This game is essentially modelled on the old coconut shy game. The cans or cups are arranged into a pyramid on the table and then knocked down one after another using the hose. This method means that each child will almost certainly hit the cans or cups, and everyone has great fun at the same time. Every year my son insists that we play Fireman´s Fun at his party!

At his seventh birthday,

we expanded the idea of Fireman's Fun to involve a course that had to be traversed blindfolded. The other children shouted instructions such as "to the right", "to the left", "higher" or "lower" to the wildly spraying blindfolded child. As no blindfolded child had managed to spray the cans off the table based on the instructions, after some time the other children helped him or her aim the hose and sprayed the cans down together.

Tip: You can stop mishaps or mischief by simply bending the hose. Turning off the tap takes too long as the water will keep flowing for a little while.

Balloon Spraying

Place: bathroom
Material: bathtub, table (which can get wet), balloon, water pistol(s)
Characteristics: fun, motor skills

If you don't want to do without water games indoors either, you can choose a variation of Fireman's Fun. A table is placed in the bathtub for this purpose. In order to avoid scratches, cloths can be put under the feet of the table. A balloon is placed on the table and sprayed away from it with a water pistol.

On my son's eighth birthday, I had given small water pistols as presents, but of course you can pass on only one water pistol, too. The size of the water pistol should be adjusted to the distance to the bathtub.

Water Fight

Place: outside
Material: bathing costumes, one empty plastic bottle with a hole in the top per child, a bucket [possibly tape]
Characteristics: fun, uproar

We normally use half litre plastic bottles and prick a hole in the tops. Squeezing these bottles creates a brilliant jet. Provide a bucket of warm water for the children to fill up their bottles, and then cold water just before the game finishes to liven things up. The exciting water fight may now begin!

Mark out a water-free boundary for children in need of a break (and indeed for anyone else wanting to stay dry, or objects that mustn't get wet), perhaps by using tape. Those on the dry side must not be sprayed, or spray anyone else.

Throwing Water Bombs

Place: hard ground, e.g. balcony with paving stones underneath
Material: balloons; [possibly chalk, bucket and plastic bottles]
Characteristics: fun

Prepare as many water balloons as you like for each child by fixing each balloon to a narrow tap and then filling it with water. Tie the water-filled balloons shut. The children may now explode their 'bombs' by throwing them – a very fun-filled activity!

As these water balloons are relatively stable, simply dashing

30

them on the ground is not usually enough to burst them. In this case the children may throw their water bombs from an elevation, balcony or terrace (if necessary arrange yourself with your neighbours) onto the pavement below. We give out the water bombs one by one at the other side of the house in order to keep the children moving and slow down the use of the balloons.

Game expansion: You could also let the children paint targets on the pavement with chalk.

For older children: Older children can also make their own water bombs. They need a bucket of water and empty plastic bottles. They fill them with water from the bucket, put a balloon over the neck of the bottle and let the water flow into the balloon. The balloon must be held by the neck of the bottle to prevent it from slipping. Then close the water-filled balloon and the water bomb is ready.

Water Bomb Fight

Place: outside
Material: bathing gear, water bomb balloons [possibly tape]
Characteristics: fun, uproar

You can buy special water bombs that are somewhat thinner than ordinary balloons and thus explode more easily. The water bomb fight is very similar in set-up to the water fight with dry zone. Yet instead of spraying each other with bottles, the children can now pelt each other with water bombs! You may like to begin this game as a water fight and then scale up the fun with a water bomb fight.

Hose Down

Place: outside
Material: bathing costumes, hose, possibly objects
Characteristics: fun, uproar

Children enjoy spraying things with a hose, running away from the jet of water or even jumping through it! The child holding the hose must not run after the other children as the hard jet of water nearest the hose mouth is

31

quite painful. If on the other hand the child spraying stays on the spot, the other children can judge the distance themselves.

Game expansion: The children could collect random waterproof objects "under threat" of the water jet.

Free Play with DIY Store Pipes

Place: outside [and inside]
Material: DIY store pipes, water access [alternatively: marbles, flummeries, small balls], possibly shovels and buckets
Characteristics: handcrafted creativity

Free Play with DIY Store Pipes is particularly suitable for boys aged three to about seven/eight. In fact, I didn't offer this free game on children's birthdays, although of course this is also possible. Rather, playing with the pipes has been my son's favourite daily game with other boys every summer for years.

The enthusiasm on a playground with a water pump was so great for the boys that they could spend hours on playing. After some time the other boys brought DIY store pipes with them, too. To distinguish between them, we labelled the pipes with a permanent marker.

Also in a garden with water hose or refillable water bucket as well as on the beach, free play with the pipes is possible. Inside or outside without water access, the pipes can be played with in such a way that marbles, flummeries or small balls are rolled through the pipes.

The only thing needed for this creative free game, which appeals especially to boys, is normal pipes, which are offered to craftsmen in every DIY store, hardware store or home-improvement center. Everything else results spontaneously from the environment and from the respective situation. Since the pipes are relatively inexpensive and extremely stable, I would like to recommend them to you.

Note: Count the pipes before you let the kids start to play, so that you will afterwards take them all back with you.

Fantasy and Story Games

Most of the following games can simply be used as tasks, but they can be even more fun if you weave a little story around them to fire the imagination.

Treasure Hunt
Place: outside, also possible indoors
Material: treasure chest (e.g. colourful glittering laminated boxes), one prize per child, prepared clues
Characteristics: adventurous, adaptable

Even small children of kindergarten age are enthusiastic treasure hunters. Hide a treasure chest containing prizes for all the children, who then look for the treasure as a group. To do this, hold up a piece of paper on which you have drawn a brief place to be guessed. The next clue is to be found at this place, and will point to a second secret location. The treasure should be 'discovered' after three or four clues. For older children, you can combine the treasure hunt with easy tasks and expand the clue stages, until the treasure hunt becomes a rally.

Paper Plate Ship
Place: outside and inside
Material: three paper plates per child; [possibly balloons and tape or boxes]
Characteristics: cooperation, imagination

In a traditional paper plate race, two groups get three paper plates each. At the starting command, a child from each group must move as quickly as possible on the paper plates without touching the ground. The children stand on two plates as they place the third plate (the one furthest away) in front of them. When a child reaches the finishing line, he or she picks up their paper plates, runs back to their group and passes the plates to the next

33

child, who then starts the course immediately. The group that finishes first wins.

As a non-competitive game, the children are to cross a raging river – together. No child is allowed to remain behind and thus get lost. The children must also keep holding hands because otherwise their ship will leak and sink ...

First of all, demonstrate to the children how they can use all three plates to move by themselves (see competitive game). Let the children try this out once. Then take away some plates – unfortunately, there is now a problem: there are no longer enough plates. Only two plates are available per child, plus a couple of additional plates for the whole group. The children must therefore act together to cross the river. How many additional plates you give the group depends on its size and how difficult you want to make the task. When the children on the river bank have joined a group with their two paper plates, the children at the back get the additional paper plates and pass them forwards. Then leave the rest of the cooperation to the children.

If you notice that the children are managing to cross the rapids well, you can throw in a couple of problems. For example, you could play a rock in the water by standing in their way and spreading out your arms and legs. Or pretend you are a tree-trunk being carried away by the current: walk slowly straight ahead through the group, and the children must avoid you. As a waterfall, push a few plates away slightly or entirely out of range.

Paper Plate Ship can be played as a single river crossing or to fetch provisions. When fetching provisions, the children are to transport a bulky box or inflated balloons stuck together with tape.

If you would like to give out prizes for Paper Plate Ship, hide them in the box or balloons.

Newspaper Boats

Place: outside and inside
Material: old newspaper
Characteristics: imagination, fosters group spirit

Traditionally known as 'Newspaper Dance', the children dance on one sheet of newspaper each, but must not touch the ground as they move. Any child who touches the ground is eliminated. When the music stops, the newspaper paper is cut in half. The winner is the last child left.

Similarly, the children must not touch the ground in the non-competitive game. The game begins with one newspaper sheet per child, but then one is removed from a particular child and the other children accommodate this child on their sheet. As soon as all children have found a stable position on the remaining sheets, another is removed. The aim is to accommodate the entire group on as few newspaper sheets as possible.

This game gets even better if you incorporate an exciting story into it. The newspaper sheets are boats; there is a thunderstorm and a large wave will capsize a boat from time to time. The shipwrecked child must be rescued by the others, but there are crocodiles or sharks in the water. No boat is allowed to drift off, so the children grab hands.

A fun newspaper fight may also ensue at the end of this game. It is advisable not to play Wrap the Mummy and Newspaper Boats consecutively, in order to add more diversity to the whole party.

Captain Hook

Warning: not suitable for particularly sensitive children
Place: inside and outside
Material: something slimy, marmalade that is not too runny, blindfold
Characteristics: exciting, weird sensations

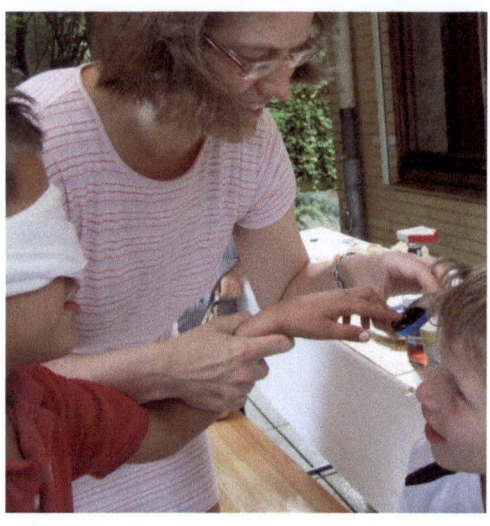

Captain Hook is particularly good after free play with a fight, as the children can now actually <u>feel</u> the results of the battle.

One child is blindfolded and another is Captain Hook. Tell them that Captain Hook was badly injured in the battle, then say to the blindfolded child: "This is Captain Hook's healthy arm" and guide his or her hand down Captain Hook's arm from shoulder to fingertips. Then say "This is Captain Hook's injured arm" and again guide the child's hand from the shoulder downwards. This time, however, Captain Hook bends his elbow and you guide the child's hand off the elbow and into thin air. To the blindfolded child, this feels as though the forearm is missing. Do the same with a healthy and an injured leg.

Finally, announce that Captain Hook has one healthy eye (very carefully let the child touch Captain Hook's closed eye) and one injured eye. For the injured eye, let the blindfolded child feel the jam or marmalade. Most small heroes really squirm at this point, which makes the other children curious to 'feel' Captain Hook too, although the surprise effect is of course lost.

You should also try the game out yourself beforehand, as it feels astonishingly real.

Guess the Animal

Place: inside and outside
Material: lots
Characteristics: performance, expression

Each child draws a lot with an animal written on it. Whisper the animal names into the child's ear if they cannot read very well yet. Use very simple animals for small children, but the older ones can deal with something more demanding. In our experience, the children may wish for several rounds of the game, which can ascend in levels of difficulty.

The children form a large circle with one child in the middle. He or she imitates his or her animal by, for example, wriggling on the floor as a snake. The other children call out to guess the animal. Young children are also allowed to make the animal noise, while older children may only use animal noises as an additional aid if the guessing goes on for too long. In this case, you may also give further clues, such as where the animal lives, or its typical behaviour. It doesn't matter which child in the group guesses the animal; there is no particular sequence for turns. Perhaps you could also give the lots a sequence number, from which only the birthday child is exempt.

Guess the Animal should only be played later on in the party if the children know each other. Most children find it great fun to stand in the middle for a while, but shy children may prefer just to guess. If so, take care not to disregard the more reserved children.

Clothes Peg Animal

Place: outside and inside
Material: at least two clothes pegs per child
Characteristics: imaginative, creative, fosters group spirit

Give the children a bag full of pegs, which they use to connect themselves into one big 'animal' featuring lots of arms, legs and heads. Will this animal be able to move without losing any body parts i.e. children? Can it possibly hop, or climb easy objects, for example over tree-trunks?

Appeal to the children's imagination.

Introduce the animal in an exciting way: you have heard on the news that a dangerous wild animal escaped from the nearby zoo ... Or invent an anxious animal that likes to hide under a table or in a bush. Perhaps it's a cuddly animal that wants to be stroked? Take your cue from the mood of the group.

Finally the animal is 'fed' i.e. all children get a small prize in the food bowl. This could be located several rooms away, or at the other end of the lawn.

Balloon Snake

Place: inside and outside
Material: at least one blown up balloon per child
Characteristics: coordinated skill, fosters group spirit, fun

One child, in this case the birthday child, is the head of the snake. One after the other the remaining children place a balloon on their belly, pressing it against the back of the child in front. When all children have formed a snake, they let go of their balloons so

that these are held in place by belly and back alone. The snake can slither forwards and backwards, but after a while the snake head goes to the back of the line.

Game expansion 1: If you want to challenge the children's skill, ask them to sit or even lie down without losing their balloons.

Game expansion 2: The child at the head of the snake may set an additional task, for example tell all children to wave their right hand, pinch their nose, clap above their heads, whistle a song and so on.

Robots

Place: outside and inside

Material: -

Characteristics: excitement through pair coordination

The children find a partner. One child is the robot, the other the robot controller. Swap after a while. To make the robot walk, the controller touches him or her on the back. The robot will now walk straight ahead until he or she is ordered to change direction right or left by a touch on the corresponding shoulder. If the controller puts a hand on the robot's head, he or she must stand still. The controllers should ensure that the robot doesn't run into anything.

Gathering Ghosts

Place: inside and outside

Material: one blindfold per child (e.g. tea towels are suitable, or cut an old sheet up)

Characteristics: foster community, playing ghosties

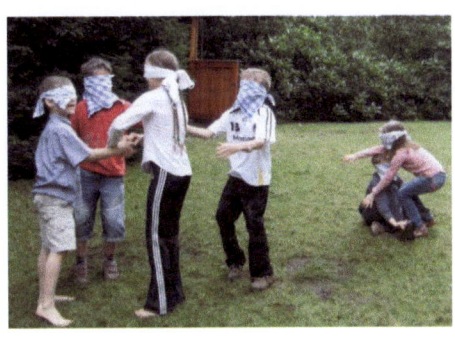

The children space out in a set area. They are blindfolded on their chosen spot and turned around a few times to lose orientation. At the start signal, the children must find each other by howling in a ghostly way. The aim of the game is for the ghosts to form a nice round circle. You can specify beforehand whether touching is allowed, or wait to see which solutions the children think up by themselves. Gathering Ghosts can also be played first with touching and then without. Any child that thinks that the group of ghosts has completed its task should stand still and stop howling. When all the children have stopped howling, they can remove their blindfolds and see how successfully they have formed the circle.

If individual children are not confident enough to walk around blindfolded, cheating is allowed. Otherwise you can tie the blindfold around their forehead, so that the child can draw it over his or her eyes a bit later on in the course of the game.

Please note: If you set up Gathering Ghosts outside, please ensure you put away any dangerous objects and get rid of any potential hazards before the game starts. Inside, always put away breakable objects as a precaution.

Hot on the Tracks
Place: inside and outside
Material: about fifteen paper plates [possibly paper cups]
Characteristics: exciting tactile experience

In this game, little detectives follow a hot track in the truest sense of the word. One child – the thief – places paper plates facing downward at a distance of approximately ten centimetres. The thief then waits at the end of the 'trail' to be caught by the detective – if he or she correctly follows this paper plate trail. The detective is then blindfolded and feels for the trail with his or her bare feet. If he catches the thief, the children join hands and the detective leads them both back with the thief as a prisoner. The detective then becomes the thief for the next child and sets a new trail.

Game Variant 1: Paper cups can be set up as obstacles, which the children must not topple over. If necessary, the detectives can feel the cups with their hands and put them upright again.

Game Variant 2: This alternative is too difficult for most children, but some do like to be challenged. For these guests, the trail is laid after they are blindfolded.

Detective and Murderer

> Age: older children
> Place: inside and outside
> Material: - [possibly lots]
> Characteristics: experience a crime, ability to use clues to solve a puzzle

One child – the detective – leaves the room. The other children then decide who the murderer is amongst themselves. This can also be decided by drawing lots, in which case nobody knows who it is. The guests now carry on a birthday party until a body suddenly falls to the floor. The murderer has struck! The detective is then fetched and must unravel the murder mystery. Will he find the murderer by his questions? All children must answer the detective's questions truthfully; only the murderer may lie.

Food Games

The following games rely on food as the main material. The games range from skill exercises, perception games to the comical and fun.

Eating Marshmallows

> Place: inside and outside at the table
> Material: one to two chocolate marshmallows per child
> Characteristics: challenging, motor skills

Eating Marshmallows is mostly played in competition i.e. who has eaten their chocolate marshmallow the quickest without using hands. Argument often ensues afterwards as to who was actually the fastest.

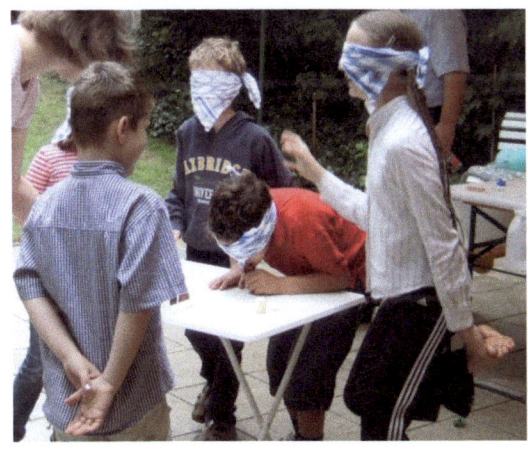

41

Instead of this, allow the children to begin at different times and set another challenge: "See whether you can eat the marshmallow with your hands behind your back and standing on one leg." It is even more difficult to do the same thing with your eyes closed! (Cheating is allowed in this game.)

Jelly in the Belly

Place: inside and outside, at the table
Material: one jelly with spoon per child, blindfold
[possibly one straw per child]
Characteristics: challenging, fun

For younger children, two guests sit opposite each other and feed each other jelly. This is quite difficult!

The principle is the same for older children, but the person feeding will be blindfolded. Then swap over. Let the children play for as long as they are having fun – the

rest of the jelly can then be eaten normally.

You can also offer the children straws to suck up the remaining jelly to make things a bit different.

Tip: Cover your carpet if you want to protect it!

Guess the Taste

Place: inside and outside
Material: small bowls or paper cups with various foods, blindfold
Characteristics: quiet, sensory perception

The little bowls are filled with different foods such as sugar, salt, flour, jam, ketchup, mustard, cocoa, chocolate sprinkles and so on. Each child should now guess the foods while blindfolded.

In order to include the children standing around, we let them each choose six bowls from a larger selection for the guessing child. Moreover, at the beginning each guessing child is allowed to place aside a bowl they did not want to try. (In our experience, most children reject mustard). With younger children, Guess the Taste can also be played without blindfolds.

Don't forget: If you would like to give out prizes for this game, then please do so for participation and not for how much the children got right.

The Flour Tower

Place: inside and outside (not when windy)
Material: a plate or board, flour, a knife, matches
Characteristics: skill, funny

The Flour Tower is best played at a table. Some flour is packed tightly into a pile on a plate and a match (no head) is placed on the top. The children take turns to cut a slab off the flour pile carefully with a knife, and push the piece aside. They should take care that the match does not roll over or fall down the pile. *When this eventually happens, however (which it will as the tower becomes ever narrower and*

43

more unstable), the child whose turn it was must fish out the match from the flour using only their mouth. A fun floury face is guaranteed!

The Flour Tower in its traditional form may cause some children to feel embarrassed by their floury face. The non-competitive version of the game gives the children the opportunity to pass, which makes the 'unavoidable' floury face totally optional. So each child in each round may choose to cut off a piece of flour or say "Pass". This means that the child is exempt from play and the turn passes to the next birthday guest.

Usually, most or all children will face the challenge to cut more flour from the dwindling pile with plenty of excitement. However, it should also be perfectly acceptable if nobody wants to fish out the match: instead, finish the game without reproof or pressure to continue.

Personally, it is my experience that children are eager to fish the match out of the flour. At one party, the game even ended in a boisterous flour fight! With the children covered in flour from top to bottom, I then went on to play Gathering Ghosts.

Stip-Stop Eating

> Place: inside and outside
> Material: during meal time
> Characteristics: fun while eating

Older children like this game during tea time. Each child takes it in turn to say "Stip-Stop!" and all the others then continually repeat the very last movement they made. If the child then says "Stop!" they must all remain dead still. Only the child who has said "Stip-Stop"  or "Stop" may continue moving. After a short time (limit if necessary) he or she says "Go!" and the other children may continue eating. It is now the next child's turn to say "Stip-Stop" and "Stop".

Snatch Sausages

Place: outside and inside

Material: clothesline, short bands, sausages or vegetarian sausages; [possibly blindfolds]

Characteristics: challenge of skill

Pull a clothesline through a room or garden or playground and tie, hanging on short bands, sausages to it. The clothesline should hang so high that the children can easily catch a sausage with their mouths without using their hands. For younger children, this is already enough of a challenge. Cheating is allowed.

Older children are allowed to do this with their eyes blindfolded. Leave it to the children if they want to try blindly.

Also for this game applies: Stay as supervision continuously with the children in the case that the clothesline loosens possibly.

Painting and Crafts

Crafts is a nice activity particularly in rainy weather and/or when you have limited space, but not all children enjoy it. Ask your child beforehand to help you find out about the guests in order to avoid disappointment. Even if the children enjoy crafts, you should consider the fun and excitement of the birthday party, and not place too much emphasis on concentration and endurance. Simple Origami patterns have proved popular.

Origami

Place: inside and outside (no wind) at the table

Material: (coloured) paper

Characteristics: quiet, making something out of paper

There are ORIGAMI books for children that offer a range of good ideas. I would advise you to try out the chosen models with your child prior to the party, in order to master the pattern and be able to judge the level of difficulty for the guests. You should be able to provide enough assistance if needed so as to guarantee a successful experience.

Making Dominoes

    <u>Place</u>: inside and outside (no wind) at the table
    <u>Material:</u> firm (coloured) paper, pens, ruler, scissor(s)
    <u>Characteristics</u>: make and play a game together

Cut out large rectangular pieces of paper for younger guests, or for older children simply draw the outlines (or let them work independently). The general rule of thumb is: the younger the child, the bigger the rectangle. Rule a line across the middle of the rectangle, producing two halves.

Paint a pattern or motif on one of the halves, and copy that exact picture onto a different rectangle half. Choose another picture for a third rectangle half, and so on. Possible pictures include geometric shapes, animals, dice dots, flowers, letters, cars, a colour, or stick men.

Make sure that the children create overlapping rectangles in order to create a domino game for all, with lots of domino pieces. The overlapping pieces are painted by two different children on the two halves of one rectangle. The children may make as many dominoes as they please.

Once the dominoes are ready to use, everyone comes together to join the pieces into a long sequence, with the matching patterns facing each other.

Play Dough

    <u>Place</u>: inside and outside at the table, access to an oven
    <u>Material:</u> flour, salt, water, bowl, paints, varnish;
    [possibly cups, rolling pin, cut-out shapes]
    <u>Characteristics:</u> creative shapes, possibly communal project

To make the play dough, mix the flour and salt in a bowl at a ratio of two to one and knead with water to form a firm, pliable dough. Let the children put the flour and salt (two cups to one) into the bowl and mix as you add water. The splashing and sludge is great fun.

The children can then shape the dough as they please, but don't expect too much! Some children will make something that is barely recognisable, but with a bit of imagination you can see something in any shape. Success with play dough is also easily had if you suggest that the children make hand or footprints.

With especially adept children, on the other hand, you can set them a joint task, such as making a zoo. Those who find animals too difficult could perhaps also contribute by making the fences.

Younger children love to make shapes out of rolled-out dough. To prevent the dough from sticking, dust the rolling pin and table with a bit of flour. You could also make a small hole in the shapes so that you can hang them up later.

In actual fact, the play dough shapes should now be left to dry for a day and then baked at approximately 50°C for one to two hours. Cracks or bubbles may form at higher temperatures from damp dough. Yet these minor flaws do not generally bother the children; sometimes they even find it amusing. For fast results at the birthday party, bake the shapes at 150°C to 200°C for 30 to 60 minutes until they become hard (they will sound hollow, and look light brown). Thicker shapes need more time than their thinner counterparts and must therefore be removed at a different time.

When the shapes have cooled, they can be painted and covered with clear varnish later on. Don't apply the paint too thickly because otherwise it will crack whilst drying. And don't forget the potential mess caused by dough and paint!

Foot Painting

Place: inside and outside on smooth ground
Material: large drawing paper (e.g. white paper tablecloth), thick wax crayons
Characteristics: unusual, motor skills

Lay large sheets of sketch paper across the floor for all the children, and weigh it down at the edges so that it doesn't slip. Each child should now stick a wax crayon between their bare toes and draw, paint or even write to their hearts' content.

Street Picture
Place: outside, dry stone floor
Material: chalk
Characteristics: quiet, creative

Let the children chalk a mutual picture on the ground! This is best in fine weather, and of course in an appropriate place. (Please consider traffic safety.)

My son often paints the paving stones leading into the garden with a welcome greeting. Doing so, he is occupied during the birthday preparations and busy preparing a cheerful welcome for his guests. So far, every single guest has found the way to the house.

Magic

Kindergarten children get excited by very simple magic tricks, so all you need to do is practise them once beforehand. Don't be surprised if the children are totally fascinated and want you to repeat the magic trick again and again. Make the magic even more exciting by giving the children colourful wands (decorated straws, for example) and let them help by saying Simsalabim or Abracadabra.

If you want to do more challenging magic for older children, you will find a huge range of tricks in specialist magic shops. Don't worry if it doesn't work out perfectly - the children will be proud that they have figured out the trick ... Perhaps you could even reveal your secrets and let the children try as well!

Disappearing Coin
Place: inside and outside
Material: coins; [possibly a wand per child]
Characteristics: surprise effect

In your right hand, show the children a coin. The children should take good note of which hand the coin is in. Then rub your left forearm (which should be bent) with the coin still in the right hand. Close your left hand at the same time. Ask where the coin is and show it as confirmation. As you rub your arm, the children say a magic word. Now there is an unfortunately mishap: you drop the coin! Discreetly pick up the coin with your left hand instead of your right, and continue your magic as before. You have conjured the coin out of your right hand! Where is it? Use your left hand to take it out of a child's sleeve, trouser leg or pocket.

Guess the Card
Place: inside and outside
Material: card game with memorable pictures [possibly one wand per child]
Characteristics: amazement at your knowledge!

Hold out the cards (somewhat covered) to a child. He or she then pulls out a card and shows it to the other children without you seeing. In the meantime, split the pack into both hands and make a mental note of the bottom-most card in your left hand. The child puts his or her card on the pile in your right hand and you put the left pile on top. To find the right card out of so many, you now need the children to say the magic word. When you then shuffle through the pile, the card you are looking for will be just before the one that you had previously noted yourself.

Keep it Casual

Even with the best of preparation, one child or another may not want to play either at the start or during the party. You should accept this, and not press the child to join in. Turning to your inner family, please calm your inner woman. She is by no means responsible for everything. It is enough if she tries to make the birthday party as good as possible. What comes out in the end is no longer her responsibility, but it will come exactly as it should come.

If a child does not join in at the beginning, you are probably dealing with a shy child. Take her or him by your side to give her or him security. Being so close to the group will ease her or his later entry to the games.

If a child abandons the game during the party, briefly ask what's wrong. It could be that she or he has an aversion to a game for whatever reason, or simply needs a break. Perhaps the child might like to take on the role of helper in order to remain part of the group, for example, he or she could help blindfold the other children when playing Gathering Ghosts and ensure that nobody bumps into anything, or trips over.

In this way you can also specifically address children, who interfere to get your special attention. Sometimes a single child needs so much attention that you should consider this need. In addition, for example, a game like **Clothespin Theft**, which focuses on one child, is also suitable. For Clothespin Theft, you give the child, who needs increased attention, ten to twenty clothespins to attach to her or his clothes. Then, the child is allowed to run away (possibly limited to a certain area), while the other children try to steal her or his clothespins. As soon as a child gets a clothespin, she or he must return it to you before stealing any more. This prevents competition between the children through comparing, who has received the most clothespins. In addition, the child running away will not be stolen too many clothespins at once, which could cause a feeling of frustration. A quieter variant of this game would be a blindfolded execution limited to little space.

Primary-school age boys (I have not experienced it with girls) like to set their own limits and show themselves to be strong by refusing to play certain games. I do not involve myself in this at all; I simply explain that participation is voluntary and then keep playing with the other children. It is my experience that the boys join in again a little later: they don't want to miss out on the fun.

If there is a positive mood overall and the children generally join in with enthusiasm, I would consider it to be a very successful birthday party!

Consider the Age of the Children

Very young children are just discovering the world, so almost everything is exciting and stimulating for them. They particularly like things that are shiny and colourful, so blowing bubbles, for example, should definitely be included at the party.

At kindergarten age, then, it is very easy to fire your guests' imagination. The children get thoroughly carried away in a story, which you can use to build up lots of excitement over the course of the party (see next chapter). I recommend presenting the birthday party games in a fantasy setting. Structured games should only have very simple rules at kindergarten age, such as "Toy Races".

Toy Races

Number of children: from 2 children
Age: kindergarten age
Place: inside and outside
Material: paper, paint box, scissors, sellotape, approx. 30 paper plates, 6 toy figures, 1 dice
Characteristics: exciting contest between the figures, without competition between the children

This game is based on the Ravensburger board game "Snails Pace Race". For an improvised birthday version, mark any 6 medium-sized figures, stuffed animals or toy cars with 6 different colours. Label a dice with the same 6 colours.

Your child can help you paint some paper in 6 different bright colours. After the paint has dried, cut out the dice surfaces and labels for the figures. Sellotape these coloured labels onto the sides of the dice and the figures. Ensure that neither the paper nor the sellotape protrudes over the edges, or the dice cannot be thrown properly. The labelling is easier with bigger dice.

Please note: if your little guests like crafts, feel free to include the preparation as part of the party.

Build 6 racetracks consisting of 5 paper plates for each course and place the toy figures before them. The length of the course can be adapted depending on the little ones' ability to concentrate: i.e. you can unobtrusively add or remove any number of paper plates later in the game.

The children now take turns to throw the dice, and the toy figure with the corresponding colour is moved forward to the next paper plate. The "fastest" figure wins.

This game therefore entails one winner and five losers – but these are the toys, not the children. The toys are not assigned to individual children, so you should make sure you do not choose toys to which any one child is especially attached. The children then develop an unbiased interest in the outcome of the contest.

At about eight or nine years old, children gradually lose their original child-like enthusiasm and become increasingly critical. They develop logical/linear, structured thinking and cannot be appealed to through imagination as much as before. This change is particularly difficult for parents, as both they and their decisions for the birthday arrangements are increasingly questioned – but without the children organising their own parties as adolescents do.

Navigating a cave was adventurous and exciting for this particular age group at my son's ninth birthday, while a five-year-old present was only confident enough to join in when accompanied by his father.

Cave Adventure

I asked the children what they need in a cave adventure so as not to get lost (compass) and to test the air for enough oxygen (candles).

As expected, nobody was well enough equipped, so the children first had to "buy" a small, old bag by playing Jumping Jack. In the bag were two half-length candles (one a replacement), matches, a compass and a clue. [**WARNING:** Do not let the children play with fire unattended]

The bag looked considerably well-worn, and with half-burned candles and matches instead of modern lighters, everything felt very adventurous. Thus equipped, the children had to find some treasure in the dark cellars of our block of flats just by candle light and the clue.

On the piece of paper I had written how many steps they should go in one direction. After about eight clues of this sort (with some discreet help from me) they had found the treasure, beaming with joy.

Other suitable games for this age group include funny games, such as The Flour Tower or Shaving Balloons.

Shaving Balloons

Age: primary school age
Place: outside and inside, somewhere that you can make a mess
Material: 1 balloon per child [plus 1-2 replacement balloons per child],
1 disposable razor per child, shaving foam, possibly covers for the floor.
Warning: please watch out for the sharp razor blades
Characteristics: deep sensitivity, fun with splashing foam

Each child blows up his balloon, which you smear with shaving foam. Give each child a disposable razor, with which they must 'shave' the balloon. The object of the game is to get rid of all the foam without popping the balloon. The foam will obviously drop on the floor, so make sure the ground is protected (by bin liners, for example).

Please note: Boys will have even more fun at this game if you link it to shaving in adulthood – the boys will then feel rather "grown up".

You should also bear in mind that peer influence increases with age. If your child's circle of friends usually plays soccer on someone's birthday, you should factor in their expectation of doing the same. It is best to ask your child how her or his friends usually celebrate birthdays, and what your child would like to do at her or his birthday party (with additional surprises from you).

A sporty alternative to soccer can be a visit to an open air swimming pool. For ten to eleven year olds, I organized a birthday party in the outdoor pool,

which they were still enthusiastic about for a long time. Bathing with water slide alternated with games from this birthday guidebook, which were held on the sunbathing lawn.

Climbing parks can also be a safe and at the same time physical and psychological challenge for older children. To what extent a climbing park is suitable for your birthday child and her or his guests should be clarified in advance, because this idea is especially appropriate for sporty, courageous children, who want to try themselves out.

Experience shows that older children like games as "Detective and Murderer", "Strung!", "Guess the Animal" and above all Rallies.

Build up the Suspense

Not only can you offer the children the described non-competitive games as individual games in themselves, but you can also link them together to build up suspense and excitement. Take care, however, not to over-strain them with too many games. On my son's seventh birthday I had very good results by weaving the following games into a story arc.

Example of a Successful Story Arc

This was in the framework of a <u>Treasure Hunt</u>. I introduced it very mysteriously with <u>Chinese Whispers</u>. With a secretive "Psst" and looking carefully around me, we put our heads together and whispered phrases like "The secret is a treasure", "The treasure is hidden" and "Do you want to know where?" etc. Finally, the children found out the location of the first clue.

This clue revealed the hiding place of the second. On it I had written what the children had to do to get there: cross a rushing river. At this point I gave them the plates for <u>Paper Plate Ship</u>. At first the children were allowed to start individually with three plates each, yet just before reaching the 'other side' I explained that the small boats were no longer safe against the strong current. "What could you do to get over the river despite that?" I asked. The children then had to turn around and exchange their little boats for a larger ship – all together.

On the second clue I painted a <u>(Balloon) Snake</u>, which the children had to battle to get to the third clue. For this, the children first had to form the huge snake, so as to then to fight it by playing <u>Balloon Stomp</u>.

The third clue led the children back over the river. Had anyone thought to anchor the paper plate boat? Unfortunately the ship had drifted off and they had to build new boats. To do this they were able to play <u>Hit the Nail on the Head</u>. Playing <u>Newspaper Boats,</u> they reached the original bank again, battling storms and pirate attacks (newspaper fight).

The fourth clue told the children that they had to follow a trail to get to the treasure. On the treasure chest was another clue reading "Warning", "Do not open!!!" and "Deadly!!!", with skulls and swords painted on it. Were the children brave enough to open the chest? They reacted uncertainly. Finally, inside it they discovered their prizes for free play, and the fantasy story came to an end.

While several games can merge into a **story arc**, the following **themed birthdays** provide a more standardised presentation. Both individual games and exciting story arcs can be set up as part of this theme.

Themed Birthdays

 You can give the birthday party a theme, such as Cowboys and Indians, fairies and elves, pirates, rallies or horses. The invitations can then be designed accordingly and the children can dress up if need be.

Tip: Have some face paint at the ready so that un-costumed children can still join in. Make-up and dressing-up is fun for most children, but if a child doesn't want to, this should be accepted.

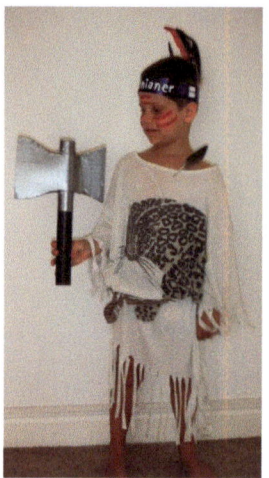

Pirates

The following games work particularly well for a pirate-themed birthday, but they are just suggestions: with a bit of imagination, any favourite game can be incorporated. Incidentally, you do not need to make all games strictly pirate-themed; it's enough to come back to it every now and then.

You could also think about adding a **treasure map** to the invitation, with directions to the party location.

Treasure Hunt: Pirates love going on treasure hunts. As already described, you can use the treasure hunt as a story arc for more games.

Newspaper Boats: Pirates spend a lot of time on the sea, and sometimes there are storms... Your little pirates have barely survived these when there is a battle straight afterwards (newspaper fight).

Chinese Whispers: Once on the Treasure Island, the pirates first have to come to an agreement. Careful, you can only whisper details of the secret treasure.

Blind Man's Buff: In a dark cave you may encounter friends, but also foes. Who will the pirates face?

Balloon Snake: There is a dangerous constrictor on the island.

Balloon Stomp: The constrictor is fought and killed. Instead of treading on them, the balloons can also be popped with pirate swords.

Captain Hook: Injuries are examined after a heavy battle.

Guess the Taste: Even pirates have to refuel from time to time. But the provisions went missing in the last battle! Looking for food in the wild is not completely danger-free ... Be careful what you find – is it edible or poisonous?!

Eating Marshmallows: Great, the pirates have found something edible!

Sack Races Tag: The pirates can only get over the deep ravine by jumping from rock to rock. There is technically no 'catching' in this, but the children will not particularly notice!

Clothes Peg Animal: What sort of monster is this? It seems quite friendly, though ... The pirates simply let it pass by.

Fireman's Fun: The route is blocked. What now?

Water Fight: Pirates are always fighting!

Buried Treasure: There's a prize for every child hidden in a sand box or soft soil. Each child is given a spoon and can dig until he or she has found a little package. This may only be opened when all children have dug theirs up.

Rally

Age: older children

Place: outside, possible anywhere – in the city, in the countryside, in the forest, by the lake ...

Material: prepared task sheets at each station, paper and pens for individual groups, set up as you please

Characteristics: spirit of adventure

In a traditional rally, the children are divided into several groups and sent off at intervals so that the teams don't overtake each other. They must then solve the tasks at individual stations and find the next one.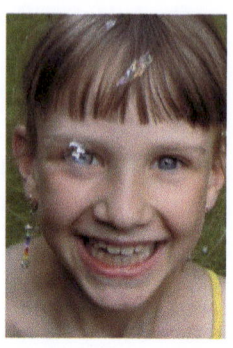

The destination should be arranged so that all children can get there, even if a group gets lost. To enable the children who have lost their way to get back into the rally before reaching the end point, you should incorporate distinctive points and street names, which they can ask passers-by. It is also recommended that each group (accompanied by adults if need be) has a working mobile and your phone number.

Usual tasks in rallies include bringing something with you, solving puzzles, writing poems, finding peculiarities on the way such as some sort of inscription, counting steps or windows and so on. If you have enough helpers, you can also incorporate games into the stations. Please don't forget, however, that it takes much longer to find a solution than to set a task so the rally should not go on for too long.

The nature of a rally is essentially retained in the non-competitive factors. *Only the competitive atmosphere between the various groups* is removed. This is relatively simple if you consider two points.

1. Setting tasks whose solutions can only be right or wrong ensure that the children find the next point - the solution is automatically checked: there is only one possible answer to enable them to find the next clue. For example, a task could be: "Count the number of steps leading up to the bridge. How many are there? Now go straight on past the same number of street lights. At the end you will find your next task under a board." Or they could solve a riddle to discover the next station.

2. All 'bring with you' and creative tasks are not undertaken in competition; instead they complement each other. For this you should divide the children into no more than three groups: blue, yellow and red. At some stations the children will find blue, yellow and red clues, each with different tasks that are put together at the end point. For example, the individual teams must paint the left, middle and right side of a building, car or animal. In order to make sure the picture fits together, lines are drawn on the edge to show participants how big their object has to be. Or the children should think of a story that ends with a sentence that is the start for the next group. Read as a whole, the story will certainly be very funny. Or each group must do a third of a puzzle that will only become complete at the destination. The first group could bring a plant with them; the second some earth and the third group does the planting at the destination. Let your creativity go wild!

Horses

While Pirates appeals more to boys, the girls at a seventh birthday party enjoyed the horse theme. The party started by **Making Hobbyhorses**. To do this, you need one stick per horse, craft material for the heads and crepe paper for the tails. The head and tail are each fixed on the stick with adhesive tape. If you live in or near the country, you can use smooth, round willow sticks. Otherwise, sticks can be bought at a DIY store.

Horse heads can be made from all sorts of materials such as wood, fabric or cardboard. It is easiest for a children's birthday if you buy ready-made kits that include instructions. Girls aged about seven and upward are able to create very nice hobbyhorses.

The first thing to do afterwards is to have a go on them, of course. Then the girls were allowed to play what I like to call **Piñata Jousting** (riding up to an item suspended in the air and breaking it open; one by one, and not against each other). To do this, hang some balloons on a clothesline and give each girl a sharpened pencil. They can then 'ride' up to the balloons and pop them.

Afterwards they had a ride in the form of a **Rally**, which also had a horse theme. In this, the girls were supposed to find a horseshoe and put together a horse puzzle, among other things. At the end of the party they were able to take their home-made horses proudly home and put them in their home 'stables'. What a pity that this wonderful birthday was over so soon!

Alternative: If the girls are younger or the hobbyhorses are too much effort, you can make little **Paper Horses**. For this you need some stiff paper (such as photo card), pens, scissors and clothespins. The horses are particularly pretty if the colour of the pegs goes well with the colour of the paper.

For younger girls, just draw simple horses without legs (perhaps by using a template) i.e. only draw the head, neck, stomach and tail. Older girls can paint their own horses. Add the eyes, mouth and mane with felt-tip pen. Then let the girls cut out the horses (if necessary with your help) and use the pegs as legs. By attaching a peg at the front and behind the stomach, this happy horse will be able to stand up perfectly.

How to Lead Non-Competitive Games Convincingly

Now that you have familiarised yourself with a whole range of non-competitive games, the question arises: do the non-competitive games appeal to you emotionally, or have you instinctively dismissed them? I ask because your honest answer to this question is important.

Do you privately incline towards non-competitive games, or do you in fact prefer competition games? Do you find competitions exciting, and consider non-competitive games fundamentally dull? If so, you will unwittingly transmit this attitude to the children and the non-competitive games will seem boring. In this case it would be more honest to admit your preference for competition and perhaps settle on a **compromise**.

For this, you could arrange **group competitions** that do not focus on the achievements of individual children. It is important that these personal triumphs get completely lost in the fun, and that individual children are not held responsible for the whole group losing. For example, if you play traditional sack races in two groups, it is much too obvious to everyone which children were fast or slow, or which even fell over.

With Flying Balloons, two or more groups can compete quite well to see which team can keep their balloons in the air the longest. As the children are all occupied at the same time, they will hardly notice their friends and if a balloon falls to the floor nobody is likely to know whose it is.

You should mix up the groups for each new game in order to keep the children unified as a whole. It is also recommended that the groups do not choose themselves in order to avoid 'being picked last' scenarios and exclusions.

The idea to compromise by introducing group competitions means that you will maintain the competitive mood, while not exposing individual children as losers.

Another suggestion for **compromise** is **elimination games**. These retain the competitive nature of the games, but with just one winner in the foreground the many losers share the same fate. Elimination games include the traditional 'Newspaper Dance' described previously, or the widely known Musical Chairs.

*In **Musical Chairs,** chairs facing outward are arranged in a row or a circle. There is one chair fewer than the number of children. The children walk or dance around the chairs while music is playing. When the music is suddenly switched off, every child must grab a chair and sit on it. The child who doesn't manage to do so is out. One chair is taken away and the game continues. The winner is the person who sits on the last chair.*

*Another elimination game is called **Spoon Story**. The children sit in a circle around a pile of spoons. There is precisely one spoon fewer than the number of children. The adult in charge begins telling a story and as soon as the word 'spoon' appears, everyone grabs one. The child who does not manage to get one is out. One spoon is removed and the story continues. The winner is the person who manages to grab the last spoon.*

In non-competitive version, no child goes out. This does not mean that the entire competitive nature of the game is lost: instead the child who does not get a spoon goes on telling the story. (If necessary, quietly give the child a bit of help). The number of spoons remains constant.

You can of course combine competitive games and non-competitive games at any time, and thus ensure that the birthday party is a colourful mix. For older children who are already used to competitive games, I would recommend carefully trying out this technique to find out how they react to the change. If you act too suddenly, the children will become uncertain and overstrained by the unusual games.

Develop Your Own Non-Competitive Games

If you like non-competitive games, the idea behind it, or have even already tried some of them out with positive results, you might like to develop your own. It's quite simple – with a little creativity!

If this idea had not yet occurred to you, I would like to encourage you now – not only do you give the children great pleasure and create a harmonious birthday mood, but you can also have a lot of fun developing them yourself.

I prepare many of these games as a surprise for my son, but we also invent some together. Children are often very creative and know best what's fun. In fact, it was my five-year-old son who largely thought up the newly-modified Pass the Potato! So you can involve your child in the process without undue concern.

If you want to develop non-competitive games yourself, there are basically two options. You can modify well-known games, or invent completely new ones – the first alternative is certainly easier to start with. Some examples have been included among the non-competitive games ideas.

To transform competitive games into non-competitive versions or invent new non-competitive games, **the following questions are important:**

1. **Do individual children play against each other (competition) or with each other (collective)?**
2. **Do whole groups play with or against each other?**

3. If the children (groups) play against each other:
   How can the game be modified, so that competition becomes community?
4. What is the appeal of the game if there is no competition?

You should also put yourself in the shoes of the 'weaker' children. How would a lesser-able child feel in the game? Will he or she feel inferior to the other children? Are individual children exposed in such a way that the others notice a "failure"?

Please note that it is all about how the <u>children</u> perceive the game, and not how you judge the situation as an adult. Even if you consider all children equally capable, one child or another may perceive themselves to be weaker than the rest nonetheless. If a child is not as confident as the others, he or she will not participate at all if their feeling of self-worth is threatened. The children's self-estimation is the determining factor, so non-competitive games by their very nature should include essentially 'weaker' children in a positive way.

Hints and Tips for a Successful Birthday Party

Weather: We celebrated my son's sixth birthday in beautiful summer weather in his grandparents' garden. Unfortunately, you can't always choose the weather you want, but you <u>can</u> choose the season with the greatest chance of fine conditions. I have noticed that some children do not mind <u>not</u> celebrating near or on their birthday. For them, it was more important to have their party outside, which as a rule is far more nerve-fraying for the parents. So if your child's birthday is around Christmas time or in the cold season, but you would like to celebrate outside, quietly think about simply shifting the birthday party to spring or summer. Perhaps there is an appropriate public holiday for your child?

Division of Tasks: Naturally I organised my son's birthday party, but my husband and the grandparents helped me with the preparations and took on responsibilities during the party. This meant that on the day I only needed to take care of the games and keep the entire flow in mind. I was able to concentrate fully on the children and attend to them without being distracted by other tasks. If possible, I would recommend that you also share some responsibility. Perhaps you could arrange this in advance with the mother or father of a birthday guest.

Decoration: The pretty decorations included balloons, garlands and street chalk pictures, which helped everyone feel warmly welcome from the outset and made the party location easy to spot from the car.

Preparing Games: For this planning procedure of preparing games is primarily the inner man responsible. All the necessary materials were prepared in advance and kept within easy reach. I wrote a list of games and laid all the accessories out on a table so as to be able to respond to the children's mood immediately without having to spend ages looking for something. I had also prepared more games than were actually needed, because the duration of the games depends on the children and can therefore only be roughly predicted. I was also able to react more flexibly to any surprises.

Game Sequence: I also considered the sequence of games, but did not stick to it too rigidly. Ice-breaker games were unnecessary because the children already knew each other from kindergarten. Games requiring more concentration were played at the start of the party, while the best surprises were saved for last so that they would stay in the guests' memory. To round off the party at both beginning and end, we played more self-contained games or group task activities.

Game Selection: I considered which games would complement each other particularly well over the course of the party, such as Fireman's Fun fol-lowed by a Water Fight. Quieter concentration and/or skill games should be alternated with more physical activities so that the party does not become too one-sided. Looking at the personality of my son and his guests, I focused more on physical exercise, for example. I also alternated predetermined games and free play. Too many games would tire the children out, while too much free play would make the party less structured and possibly too ordinary for a birthday.

Children's Wishes: I tried to offer a wide variety of games in order to make the party very diverse and thus cater to each child's taste. To do this, I responded to individual requests, but tried not to lose sight of the group as a whole. So for instance a child asked me to play a certain game, in which the others showed little interest. I cheered the child up by telling him he could certainly play his favourite game at his own birthday party.

Leadership Style: I tried to cater to respective needs and respond to the current mood of the children, instead of imposing my own vision of which party games should be played. At the same time, I made sure I retained control of determining the framework of the birthday and guided it accordingly. This is a balancing act that every play leader must judge for him or herself. For this, you should also pay attention to the balance between your inner women and your inner men.

Guest Number: There were a total of eight infant school children at my son's sixth birthday party; five boys and three girls. The best experiences have been with manageable groups of six to eight children. Up to twelve children is recommended if you would like the birthday guests to be a united group, as there is a tendency for bigger numbers to form subgroups.[1] This may be perfect for a rally,  for example, but you should remember to plan games that suit the number of guests.

The Sixth Birthday: We began with a barbecue at around half past one because everyone was still hungry. After that, I opened the afternoon of games with the generally well-known Beat the Pot. The prizes were planes to shoot with elastic. This kept the children busy in merry free play for quite a while.

Afterwards I had planned to play Pass the Potato to get the children together again, but the guests who had attended the previous year obviously remembered Fireman´s Fun rather fondly so we played that by general request! The children put on the bathing costumes they had brought and went on to have a water fight after the game had finished.

Having thoroughly let off steam, the children then wanted to play Pass the Potato for which everyone got a bird whistle as a prize. Then the children made an origami car – with a little help!

After these quiet activities, the children were allowed to let off steam again and play Sack Race Tag. Prizes were Modelling Balloons, and the children selected their favourite colour. My husband took charge of making the shapes, which were mainly swords by the children's request. Obviously the swords were then tried out immediately: using balloons meant that the danger of injury was happily slight!

---

[1] Vgl. W.Berner, Jugendgruppen organisieren, Ein Handbuch für Gruppenleiter und Mitglieder, Reinbek bei Hamburg 1983, S.106f.

There was still time for Newspaper Boats with a Newspaper Battle, before we came to a surprise: a soap bubble pistol. Each child was allowed to

have a piggy-back ride on an adult and blow bubbles, which the other children caught.

At last came the cake. I had wanted to gather the children together again, but most of them were not hungry and ate only briefly before going back to their fliers. Only drawing lots for the party bags brought them all back together and became the official end of the party. The children were picked up at six o'clock. This also proved to be a popular time for other parents, because a late dinner with possibly over-excited children can be rather tiring.

Outcome of the Sixth Birthday Party: As my son was falling into bed totally exhausted, he sighed: "What a brilliant day. What a pity my birthday is already over; next year I want it to be just the same!"

Acknowledgements

Special thanks must go to my husband and my son, without whom this book would never have been possible. I would also like to thank Dr. Margit Maronde-Heyl (certified childcare professional, and mother to a daughter) who took an experienced look at my manuscript and added her own ideas and suggestions. Last but not least, I would also like to thank all those, who agreed to the publication of their photos, which were originally taken for private purposes only.

Feedback on these private birthday parties was so positive that I was encouraged to write this book. May it give you lots of suggestions and ideas for many wonderful birthday parties to come – I wish you harmonious children's birthdays full of joy and lots of fun.

Hamburg, July 2007   Ayleen Hadenfeldt

The first edition appeared as "Children's Birthday Parties: No Losers" by Dr. Ayleen Birgit Hadenfeldt, ISBN 978-3-8370-0672-8. This second revised edition adds in particular the new chapter "Consider the Age of the Children".

Berlin, July 2009   Ayleen Scheffler-Hadenfeldt

English edition translated by S.T. Paterson: Some of the games listed here are universal, but any cultural differences have been clarified where appropriate.

Berlin, April 2010   Ayleen Scheffler-Hadenfeldt

In connection with my name change, I have published all my books new as Ayleen Lyschamaya. In addition, BoD's color printing has been improved, so this edition now contains color images. I've also added more games and the chapter "Children's Birthday as Inner Family Birthday Party", translated by myself.

Berlin, June 2019   Ayleen Lyschamaya

Ayleen Lyschamaya

Ayleen Lyschamaya / Dr. rer. pol. Ayleen Birgit Scheffler-Hadenfeldt, born 1966 in Hamburg (Germany), is business graduate with a doctorate in international taxation.

Since 2009 she has a practice as an alternative practitioner for psychotherapy in Berlin. This has meanwhile become the focus of the worldwide spread of the Final-Enlightenment.

Ayleen Lyschamaya is the founder of the inner family as the human psyche and derived a concept for Spiritual Psychotherapy from it, which for the first time harmoniously combines psychotherapy and spirituality.

In addition, she expanded EMDR to "Spiritual EMDR", added "EMDR for Babies" and developed the Guilt feelings deletion – live love – approach© (Guilt feelings dll-practice©). In particular the latter now enables people to establish the connection from Divine to earthly in their consciousness and thus to experience self-love and the higher level of awareness of the New Age.

Ayleen Lyschamaya teaches on a completely new level the whole spiritual path to the Final-Enlightenment respectively New Age Enlightenment. Thus, as project *Loving Earth,* she leads humanity into the New Age.

Further information about Ayleen Lyschamaya:
https://new-age-enlightenment.com/ayleen-lyschamaya/

For the healthy arrival of the soul on earth

EMDR for Babies: A parents' guide for your baby's first year of life by Ayleen Lyschamaya; English Edition translated by S.T. Paterson; ISBN-13: 9783738626117

Books on Demand Shop:
https://www.bod.de/buchshop/emdr-for-babies-ayleen-lyschamaya-9783738626117

With *EMDR for Babies*
- promote healthy development
- process the birth trauma
- calm crying babies
- cure disturbed bonding
- prevent ADHD and ADD
- train perception

EMDR for Babies is natural, easy to perform and effective. Step by step you will learn how to solve problems at the age of 1 and how to optimally promote the development of your baby – for a happy future together.

The original EMDR technique by Francine Shapiro was further developed by Ayleen Lyschamaya into the EMDR parents' school for babies.

With YouTube video to illustrate the further developed EMDR technology.

https://new-age-enlightenment.com/emdr-for-babies-original/

Series: *Ayleen Lyschamaya – New Consciousness*

Volume 1: *Spiritual Psychotherapy: the inner family*
    The basic work on the inner family
    The standard work on Spiritual Psychotherapy

Volume 2: *Spiritual EMDR*
    Feelings as a spiritual way to expand one's consciousness

Volume 3: *Completely dissolving feelings of guilt*
    Guilt feelings deletion – live love – approach©
    (Guilt feelings dll-practice©)

Volume 4: *The complete spiritual path*
    The Spiritual Guide Ayleen about the Final- Enlightenment
    The basic work on the new spirituality

Volume 5: *Spiritual houseboat holiday in Holland*
    Consciousness shaping with her boyfriend (travelogue)

Volume 6: *Healing the world through consciousness development for India*
    Transformation of Buddhism and Hinduism (travelogue)

Volume 7: *Preview: Japan trip with her boyfriend* (travelogue)

The books in this series will be translated into English. You can find out, which books have already been published in English, on my website.
https://new-age-enlightenment.com/books-spiritual-path/

Series: *Ayleen Lyschamaya – New Consciousness*, Volume 1:

The basic work on the inner family
The standard work on Spiritual Psychotherapy

Spiritual Psychotherapy: the inner family
by Ayleen Lyschamaya;
English translation is in progress (state 6/2019)

Ayleen Lyschamaya with this guide is the founder of the concept of the inner family as human psyche and gives Spiritual Psychotherapy an integrated basis.

The basic work on the inner family:
The inner child makes up only one third of the human psyche, plus the inner woman and the inner man.

Also non-therapists will better understand themselves and other people with this background knowledge. An entire chapter explains the typical entanglements in relationships. If one knows the personality specific basic patterns, partnerships and also all other kinds of relationships can be arranged more positively.

The standard work on Spiritual Psychotherapy:
For the first time the individual western psychotherapies and different spiritual approaches are combined in such a way to a total concept that this knowledge can be converted in each kind of psychotherapy immediately practically.

The basic knowledge of the transcendent human being with her/his inner family is conveyed across all methods, and the holistic development of this person is also addressed. For the first time, psychotherapy and spirituality are not mixed, but integrated into a completely new overall concept.

With explanatory YouTube Video.

Games Index

The games in *italics* are *competitive*. The rest of the games are non-competitive, but often have slightly different rules from the traditional games (see game descriptions).

<u>Page:</u>

Balloon Footy	20
Balloon Snake	38
Balloon Spraying	29
Balloon Stomp	25
Beat the Pot	15
Blind Man's Buff	16
Blowing Cotton Wool Balls	16
Buried Treasure	57
Captain Hook	36
Catching Soap Bubbles	14
Cave Adventure	52
Chinese Whispers	11
Clothes Peg Animal	37
Clothespin Theft	50
Detective and Murderer	41
Disappearing Coin	48
Eating Marshmallows	41
Egg and Spoon Races	*13*
Figuring out the Puzzle	12
Fireman's Fun	28
Flying Balloons	20
Foot Painting	47
Free Play	9
Free Play with DIY Store Pipes	32
Gathering Ghosts	39
Guess the Animal	37
Guess the Card	49
Guess the Taste	43
Hanging up Laundry	18

Hideout Land	14
Hit the Nail on the Head	18
Horses	59
Hose Down	31
Hot on the Tracks	40
Jelly in the Belly	42
Keep your Distance	26
Making Dominoes	46
Making Hobbyhorses	59
Making Paper Horses	60
Modelling Balloons	67
Musical Chairs	*62*
Music Stop	22
Newspaper Boats	35
Newspaper Dance	*35*
Opening Presents	23
Origami	45
Paper Plate Races	*33*
Paper Plate Ship	33
Pass the Cotton Wool Ball	17
Pass the Matchbox	17
Pass the Potato	13
Piñata Jousting	59
Pin the Tail on the Donkey	12
Pirates	56
Play Dough	46
Playful Battle	9
Rally	58
Robots	39
Sack Catchers	27
Sack races	*26*
Sack Races Tag	26
Sardines	24
Secret Hand Pressure	11
Shaving Balloons	53
Snatch Sausages	45
Sort Chaos Circle	21
Speed Snake	19

Spin the Bottle 22
Spoon Story 62
Stip-Stop Eating 44
Street Picture 48
Strung! 24
The Flour Tower 43
Throwing Water Bombs 30
Toy Races 51
Treasure Hunt 33
Unravelling a Human Ball of Thread 21
Waggle Balloon 28
Water Bomb Fight 31
Water Fight 30
Wrap the Mummy 23